Journey
Around The Nation

EDUCATIONAL
IMPRESSIONS

Written by
Charlotte S. Jaffe

The purchase of this book entitles
the buyer to exclusive reproduction
rights. Permission to reproduce
these pages is extended to the
purchaser only.

ISBN 0-910857-06-7

Copyright © Charlotte Jaffe   1984

EDUCATIONAL IMPRESSIONS, INC.
Hawthorne, New Jersey 07507

Cover Design and Illustrations by Emilie Doyle

Teaching Guide

The activities that follow are a challenging and fun way to have your students learn about the United States and share their knowledge with parents, students, and community. The lessons may be used with gifted learners in pull-out programs, self-contained classes or with students in regular classrooms.

The book is written in an outline-type format that guides the students in selecting a state to study and in completing an independent research project. A special feature of the book is the Creative Thinking section, which provides many opportunities for the students to develop higher level thinking skills. Section V provides an optional way of using the material in simulation game format. Based on Bloom's Taxonomy and Williams' Model, skills such as Fluent Thinking, Flexible Thinking, Originality, Risk Taking, Analysis, and Evaluation are stressed.

Section I. MAP SKILLS

This section contains introductory map skills activities. Teachers may supplement this information by allowing the students to explore classroom maps and globes. The students should have a basic knowledge of United States geography before starting their "Journey Around The Nation."

Section II. RESEARCH SKILLS

The activities in this section provide basic guidelines that enable students to organize and develop their research skills. Teachers should provide opportunities for students to examine school and community resources. The SELECTION SHEET asks the students to make three study choices and to indicate their selections by 1st, 2nd and 3rd preferences. This is done to avoid duplication of choices so that the States Fair will have more varied representation. The RESEARCH SHEETS are to be kept in the students' folders and used to collect information. Students may add other shapes and categories for special research information. The research information on these sheets will

Educational Impressions, Inc.

be helpful to the students in a variety of activities through-out their "Journey Around The Nation." Most of the activities in this section are self-explanatory. The teacher may choose to have the students make a cardboard flag or map from their initial sketches on the activity pages. Their vocabulary chart may be enlarged on poster paper and displayed on a bulletin board. "Send A Letter" makes use of the information that is provided in the Reference Section of this book and teaches the students another method of obtaining information.

Section III. <u>CREATIVE THINKING SKILLS</u>

The activity pages in this section challenge the students to use their imagination as well as make decisions and solve problems. The skills are open-ended and the teacher may select the activities that are best suited to the level of the class. Students may work independently or cooperatively on these activities.

Section IV. <u>STATES FAIR</u>

The States Fair is the exciting culmination of the students' "Journey Around The Nation." The activities in this section provide step-by-step preparation for the Fair. Teachers may choose to include any or all of the activities. Parents and students from other classes may be invited to view the results of the students' efforts. Included in this section are: thank-you notes, certificate of participation, and an evaluation report.

Section V. <u>REFERENCE MATERIALS</u>

The Reference Section contains many handy resources that can be utilized throughout the "Journey Around The Nation." There are also instructions for a simulation game format. A pretest is included in this section.

I hope you and your students enjoy your journey!

Charlotte S. Jaffe

Educational Impressions, Inc.

TABLE OF CONTENTS

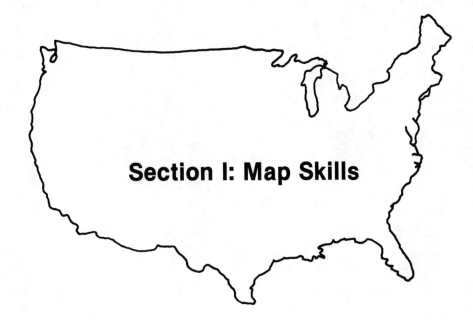

Section I: Map Skills

ALL KINDS OF MAPS!

Here is a brainstorming activity for you to complete! Within ten minutes, list as many different kinds of maps as you can! Think of the many ways that you and your family have been helped by maps. After the time is up, circle your most unusual answer.

1.

2.

3.

4.

5.

6.

7.

8.

9.

10.

11.

12.

13.

14.

Educational Impressions, Inc.

BE A MAP DETECTIVE

The lines of latitude and longitude help us to accurately locate places on a map. Latitude lines run east and west. The most important latitude line is the equator, which is half-way between the north and south pole and is numbered 0 degrees. The other lines of latitude show distances that are north and south of the equator. Longitude lines run north and south. The most important longitude line is the prime meridian. It is numbered 0 degrees longitude. All other longitude lines measure distances that are east and west of the prime meridian. Try to locate the states listed below by their latitude and longitude readings. Use the map to find your answers. Example: 40° N. latitude and 75° W. longitude? Answer: New Jersey.

1. 105° W. 35° N. _____

2. 95° W. 45° N. _____

3. 80° W. 35° N. _____

4. 85° W. 45° N. _____

5. 110° W. 35° N. _____

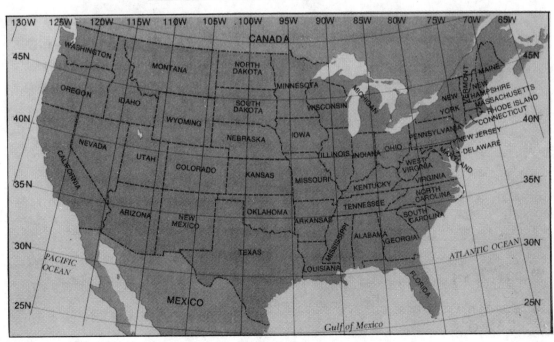

9

IT'S ABOUT TIME!

The continental United States has four <u>time zones</u> that are divided by vertical lines called <u>meridians</u>. From east to west, the time zones are: EASTERN STANDARD TIME, CENTRAL STANDARD TIME, MOUNTAIN STANDARD TIME, and PACIFIC STANDARD TIME. Eastern is one hour earlier than Central; Central is one hour earlier than Mountain, and Mountain is one hour earlier than Pacific. Alaska is located within three time zones. They are: Yukon Time, Alaska Time, and Bering Time. Hawaii is in the Alaska Time Zone.

If it is 4 o'clock in the afternoon in New York, it will be 3 o'clock in the afternoon in Illinois, and 2 o'clock in the afternoon in Colorado! What time would it be in Oregon? Look at the map below and answer the questions below it.

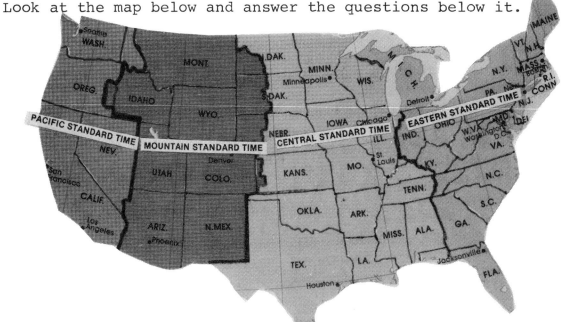

1. If it is 6 o'clock in the evening in Texas, what time is it in Oregon? _____ Virginia? _____ Utah? _____
2. If it is 1 o'clock in the afternoon in Wisconsin, what time is it in your research state? _____
3. You live in the state of Georgia. You wish to call your cousin in Arizona. If it is 10 o'clock in the morning in Georgia, what time will it be in Arizona? _____

10

FINDING DISTANCES

Miles

0   480

A map can help you find the distance between two places. Look at the map scale to find out how many miles each inch on the map stands for. Take a ruler and measure the distance between two locations. Since one inch on the map stands for 480 miles, multiply the number of inches between locations by 480 to get your answer. EXAMPLE: Since Carson City, Nevada, is one inch away from Salt Lake City, Utah, on the map, the distance between the cities is about 480 miles. Use the map to answer the questions below.

1. On the map, two inches would be equal to how many miles?
   _____

2. On the map, ½ inch would be equal to how many miles?
   _____

3. Find the distance between Austin, Texas, and Little Rock, Arkansas. _____

4. Find the distance between the capital city of the state in which you live and Linclon, Nebraska. (Choose another city if you live in Nebraska!) _____

5. How many inches on the map do you measure between Miami, Florida, and Des Moines, Iowa? _____

Educational Impressions, Inc.

POLITICAL MAPS

Political maps are used to show boundaries. The political map on this page shows where the American people live. The nation is divided by state boundaries. Within each state, the capital city is marked with a star, and other important cities are shown with dots. Read the map and answer the questions on the bottom of the page.

1. What is the capital of Texas? _____

2. What states border Colorado? _____

3. What state is north of Oregon? _____

4. Name two important cities in California. _____

5. What state is northwest of Nevada? _____

6. What states border Alabama? _____

7. What is the capital of Ohio? _____

USING ROAD MAPS

The most often used type of map is the road map. It keeps
us from getting lost and helps us to select the best routes.
Here is a road map of our northwestern states. The heavy lines
indicate turnpikes or interstate roads. Look carefully at the
map and answer the questions below.

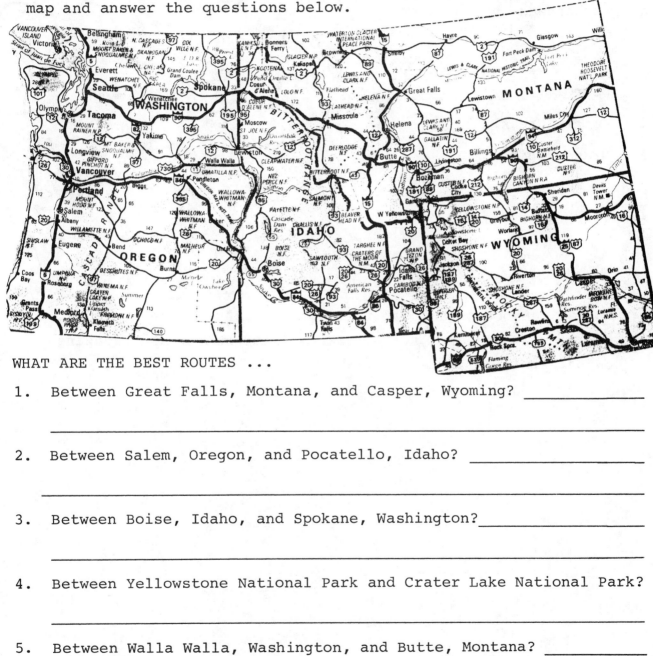

WHAT ARE THE BEST ROUTES ...

1. Between Great Falls, Montana, and Casper, Wyoming? _____
    _____

2. Between Salem, Oregon, and Pocatello, Idaho? _____
    _____

3. Between Boise, Idaho, and Spokane, Washington?_____
    _____

4. Between Yellowstone National Park and Crater Lake National Park?
    _____

5. Between Walla Walla, Washington, and Butte, Montana? _____
    _____

MAKE A PRODUCT MAP

On the right, you will see a product map of the state of Michigan. By reading this map carefully, you will be able to answer the questions below.

What Are The Leading Products Of:

1. Detroit? _____

2. Battle Creek? _____

3. Grand Rapids? _____

4. Muskegon? _____

5. Traverse City? _____

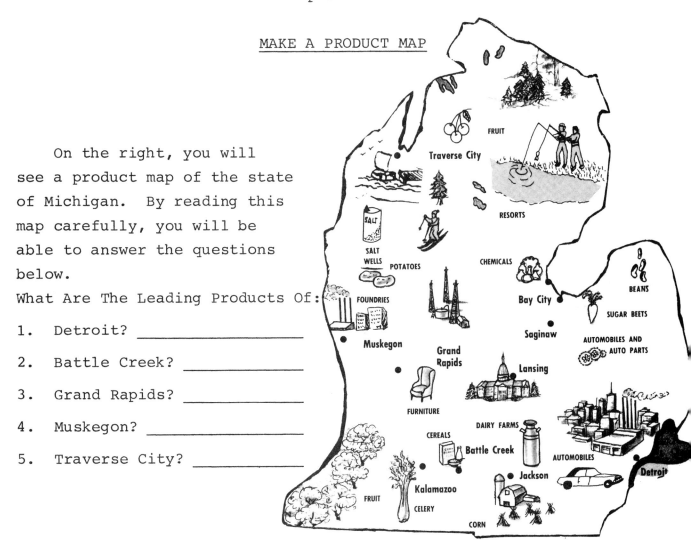

On the bottom half of this activity page, make a product map of your research state. Sketch pictures or use magazine cutouts to illustrate your map.

U.S. GEOGRAPHY GAME

Here is a game to help you and your classmates learn about United States geography! Divide the class into two or more teams. Each player takes a turn selecting a mystery state. Example: "Name a western state that is bordered by only two other states." Answer: Washington. The team that answers first gets the point! If there is no correct answer on the first clue, another clue must be provided. Use the political map in this section of the book or a large classroom map of the United States.

Write your mystery state clues in the space below. Add a sense of humor to your clues! For example: Which state is round at both ends and high in the middle? Answer: oHIo!

15

DIRECTIONS CAN BE FUN TO LEARN!

There are four basic direction words that help us to read flat maps. They are NORTH(N), SOUTH(S), EAST(E), and WEST(W). They tell us directions on the earth.

A "compass rose" is usually on a flat map to show directions:

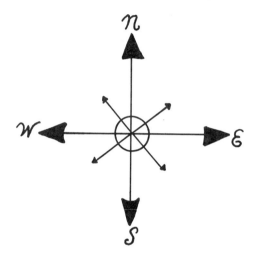

Fill in the missing directions below. Use N for North, S for South, E for East, and W for West.

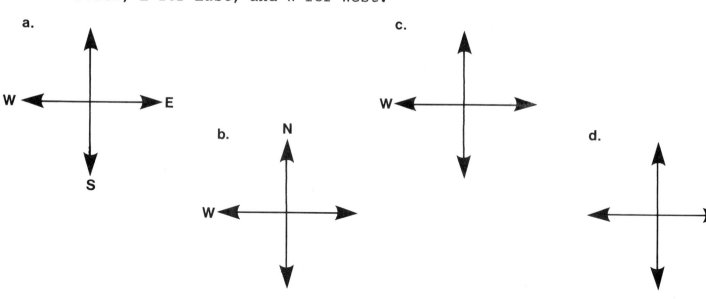

Educational Impressions, Inc.

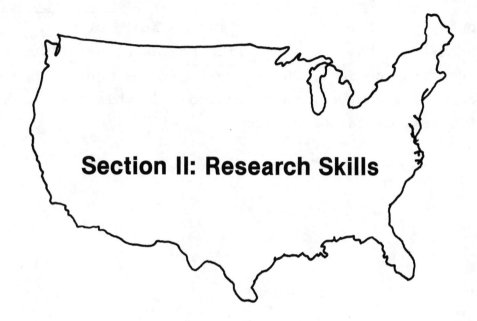

Section II: Research Skills

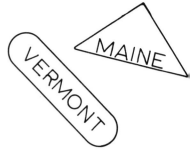

JOURNEY AROUND THE WORLD
SELECTION PAGE

We are about to begin our journey across the United States.
We will travel through small towns and large cities - past flat
farm areas and majestic mountain peaks. We will meet many kinds
of people engaged in a great variety of occupations. Let's start
at the beginning! We live in the town/city of _____
in the county/parish of _____ in the state of _____.
Decide on a state that you would like to research! Place a ◯
around your first choice. Put a ☐ around your second choice
and put a △ around your third choice. In this way, each student will have a different assignment.

ALABAMA	LOUISIANA	OHIO
ALASKA	MAINE	OKLAHOMA
ARIZONA	MARYLAND	OREGON
ARKANSAS	MASSACHUSETTS	PENNSYLVANIA
CALIFORNIA	MICHIGAN	RHODE ISLAND
COLORADO	MINNESOTA	SOUTH CAROLINA
CONNECTICUT	MISSISSIPPI	SOUTH DAKOTA
DELAWARE	MISSOURI	TENNESSEE
FLORIDA	MONTANA	TEXAS
GEORGIA	NEBRASKA	UTAH
HAWAII	NEVADA	VERMONT
IDAHO	NEW HAMPSHIRE	VIRGINIA
ILLINOIS	NEW JERSEY	WASHINGTON
INDIANA	NEW MEXICO	WEST VIRGINIA
IOWA	NEW YORK	WISCONSIN
KANSAS	NORTH CAROLINA	WYOMING
KENTUCKY	NORTH DAKOTA	

Educational Impressions, Inc.

RESEARCH SHEET I

ALL ABOUT THE STATE OF _____

BY_____

MOUNTAINS AND RIVERS

FAMOUS PEOPLE

LANDMARKS

RESEARCH SHEET II

ALL ABOUT THE STATE OF _____

MAJOR
INDUSTRIES

BY_____

IMPORTANT PRODUCTS

HISTORICAL EVENTS

1. DATE ADMITTED TO UNION_____

Educational Impressions, Inc.

FAMOUS PEOPLE

Select a person from your research state who has made an outstanding contribution to the nation or world. This person may have achieved fame in politics, music, art, science, literature, or any other field. Look in the library for information about the person. Write your report on the bottom of this page and share your findings with your classmates!

YOUR REPORT

Name of famous person_____

Date of birth_____

Name of state_____

Outstanding contributions_____

_____

_____

_____

Other information about the person's life_____

_____

_____

_____

_____

_____

_____

_____

_____

_____

Educational Impressions, Inc.

SEND A LETTER!

In the Reference Section of this book you will find the names and addresses of Chamber of Commerce Offices. Find the name and address that will help you learn more about your research state, and then write a letter asking for information. A sample letter is written below; however, you may compose your own in order to request specific information.

SAMPLE LETTER

525 Andrews Ave.
Philadelphia, PA 19117
December 11, 1983

Dear Sirs:

My name is Peter Stevenson. I am in the fourth grade at the R. J. Scott School. Our class is learning about the United States. My assignment is the state of Arizona. Please send me maps, photographs, posters, or any other information that you may have available. Thank you for your help.

Sincerely,

Peter Stevenson

Write your first draft of a letter in the space below. Then copy it over in good form on another piece of paper.

_____

_____

_____

_____

_____

_____

_____

STATE LANDMARKS

A landmark may be a famous building, structure, monument, or geographical feature that has special significance to the nation or to the area in which it is located. The Statue of Liberty, Mount Rushmore, and the White House are examples of famous landmarks. Choose a special landmark from your state to describe in this activity.

THE SPECIAL LANDMARK IS:_____

LOCATED IN THE STATE OF:_____

SKETCH OR PHOTO OF LANDMARK:

Why is the landmark important?_____

_____

On another sheet of paper, make a larger picture of the landmark and color it. Use it as part of a collage or bulletin board mural combined with those of your classmates.

Educational Impressions, Inc.

MAP YOUR STATE

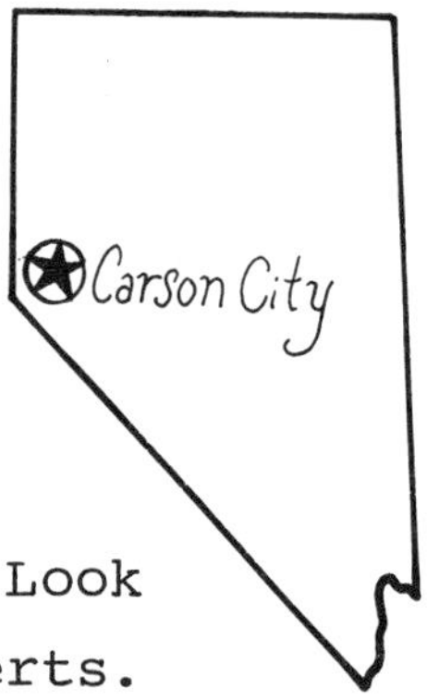

Carson City

Locate a map of your state in a reference book. Look carefully for rivers, cities, mountain ranges, or deserts. Copy the outline of your state map in the space below. Add the names of the important cities and geographical features to your map. Be sure to mark your state capital with a star. After you have made your outline in pencil, go over it with crayon or marker. For an extra challenge, mount your map on heavy cardboard and cut it into jigsaw puzzle shapes. Exchange with your classmates and solve.

THE STATE OF_____MAP

Educational Impressions, Inc.

NICKNAMES

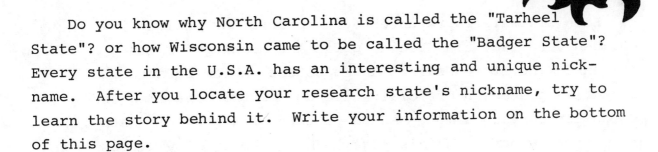

Do you know why North Carolina is called the "Tarheel State"? or how Wisconsin came to be called the "Badger State"? Every state in the U.S.A. has an interesting and unique nickname. After you locate your research state's nickname, try to learn the story behind it. Write your information on the bottom of this page.

My state:_____

State nickname:_____

How the state got its nickname:_____

_____

_____

_____

_____

_____

_____

_____

_____

_____

_____

_____

_____

Educational Impressions, Inc.

STATE FLAGS AND SEALS

Each state is represented by a colorful and uniquely designed flag that has special pride and meaning for its citizens. The state seal is an important emblem because it is usually placed on official state documents. The flag and seal often contain a motto and a picture of a state industry, product or symbol. On this page, make a sketch of your research state's flag and seal, and try to learn the meaning of the colors and symbols on them.

STATE FLAG

STATE SEAL

Educational Impressions, Inc.

SPORTS FAN SPECIAL!

Write a sports information column about your state's recreational facilities. Include some of the following information:

1. Describe the popular forms of recreation in your state.

2. List the location of recreational areas in your state. Examples: national parks, rivers and lakes, mountain areas.

3. List the names of outstanding sports teams in your state.

4. List the names of famous athletes who play or reside in your state. Describe their achievements.

SPORTS NEWS FROM THE STATE OF _____

_____

_____

_____

_____

_____

_____

_____

_____

_____

_____

_____

Educational Impressions, Inc.

OUR NATIONAL PARKS

As American citizens, we are very fortunate to have so
many national parks to visit and enjoy. Some parks are
located in wilderness areas and others, like Independence
National Park in Philadelphia, are located in the middle of
a city! Yellowstone National Park, established in 1872, was
the first national park. Locate a national park that is in
your research state or nearby. Describe it in the space below.
What sights will await visitors? What recreational facilities
are available? Give the park's exact location.

NAME OF NATIONAL PARK:_____

_____

_____

_____

_____

_____

_____

_____

_____

_____

_____

_____

VOCABULARY DISCOVERIES

As you are gathering information about your research state, you will discover many new words that describe your state in some way. These words may define a special geographical feature, special cultural or recreational activities, regional occupations, or regional foods. You are sure to uncover many such words in your research work. Write your vocabulary discoveries on the bottom of this sheet along with their definitions. When you have completed your list, share it with your classmates. Your teacher may wish to compile the words into a class booklet.

Example: LOUISIANA

VOCABULARY WORD	DEFINITION
parish	Name given to the counties in the state of Louisiana.

Add your words here!

Educational Impressions, Inc.

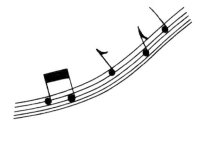

MUSICAL STATES

Many states have had popular musical songs written about them. Can you recall any? "California, Here I Come," "The Tennessee Waltz," and "Nothing Could Be Finer Than To Be In Carolina" are favorite examples. Some states have lesser known state songs. Try to locate the title and lyrics for one of your research state's songs and write it in the space below. Learn the music and sing or play it at the States Fair.

MY STATE SONG

_____

_____

_____

_____

_____

_____

_____

_____

_____

_____

_____

_____

_____

_____

_____

_____

_____

Educational Impressions, Inc.

NATIVE AMERICANS

America was once inhabited by tribes of Indians who built civilizations in different parts of our country. The Eastern Woodland Indians lived in the area from Maine to Florida from the Atlantic Ocean to the Mississippi River. The Plains Indians lived west of the Mississippi and moved around the sea frequently. The Southwest Indians were found in the high regions of Arizona and New Mexico. The Seed Gatherers wandered through the area from Nevada to Eastern California and the Northwest Fishermen inhabited the Pacific Coastal area in Oregon and Washington.

Using the reference information that you uncover, name a tribe of Indians that inhabited your state and briefly describe their civilization in the space below. What kinds of homes did they have? What kinds of food did they eat? What were their main occupations? How did they get along with neighboring tribes?

NAME OF STATE_____   NAME OF INDIAN TRIBE_____

INFORMATION

_____
_____
_____
_____
_____
_____
_____
_____
_____
_____

Educational Impressions, Inc.

SHOE BOX SCENES

Bring a shoe box, gift box, or small cardboard box to school. Create an imaginary scene of your state. Cut out a backdrop from travel folders or draw your own. Place clay or cardboard figures in the scene. Label your scene to show what is happening. In the space below, draw a sketch of your idea.

MAKE A BIBLIOGRAPHY!

A bibliography contains a list of books or other materials (pamphlets, films, filmstrips, etc.) which were used to gather information about your state. Start your own bibliography in the space below. Use the category headings to help you organize it.

Name of Book	Author	Publisher	Copyright Date	Pages Used

Educational Impressions, Inc.

Section III:

Creative Thinking Skills

Educational Impressions, Inc.

SPIN A TALE

Perhaps you have wondered how a city, town, or river in your research state got its name? Some names are derived from special geographical features or reflect the state's early settlers. Other names are more difficult to explain. Consider names such as Paradise, Texas; Opportunity, Washington; or Deadwood, South Dakota!

If you cannot determine the origin of a place, create a tall tale to explain it! Stretch your imagination and add a sense of humor to your tale!

NAME   TALE OF ORIGIN

Educational Impressions, Inc.

CREATE A PICTURE POSTCARD

Imagine that you and your family are visiting the state of _____. Send a picture postcard to someone back in your home town. Describe your visit in words on the message part of the card and draw a picture of a special part of your trip on the picture side!

Draw your picture here

Write your message   Write the address

Educational Impressions, Inc.

HEADLINE HISTORY

"TEA PARTY HELD IN BOSTON, MASS."
"GOLD DISCOVERED IN CALIFORNIA"

Read about an important historical event that occurred in your research state. Describe it in a news report with an appropriate headline. Remember to use the five W's and an H, (who, what, where, when, why and how) to report the important and exciting events in your story. Share your news report with your classmates.

MY HEADLINE: _____

_____

_____

_____

_____

_____

_____

_____

_____

_____

_____

_____

_____

_____

Educational Impressions, Inc.

WHAT STATE AM I?

Here is a riddle about a state in the U.S.A. The first clue is GENERAL and the fourth clue is more SPECIFIC. Try to solve the riddle and then create two of your own! Share your riddles with your classmates.

CLUE 1.   Cattle and sheep are important in this state.

CLUE 2.   One fourth of the nation's oil is produced here!

CLUE 3.   The Alamo and the Rio Grande are found in this state.

CLUE 4.   The "Lone Star State" became our 28th state.

WHAT STATE AM I? _____.

Create your own riddles here!

IF I WERE GOVERNOR...

Each state has its own government, with its own constitution and its own governor. Courts are also a part of each state government. Look up the following information about your state government.

NAME OF STATE_____

CAPITAL CITY_____

NAME OF GOVERNOR_____

Use your imagination to complete the second half of this activity. If you were the governor of your research state, what improvements would you make? What new laws would you like to see enacted? Remember, the state government has the power to decide what local governments can and cannot do. Write your ideas in the space below.

If I were governor,_____

_____

_____

_____

_____

_____

_____

_____

_____

_____

Educational Impressions, Inc.

CREATE A LICENSE PLATE

Each state has a uniquely designed automobile license plate. The license plates often display state nicknames, slogans, or pictures of a state. Research your state's license plate and draw it in the space below. Be sure to use the correct colors.

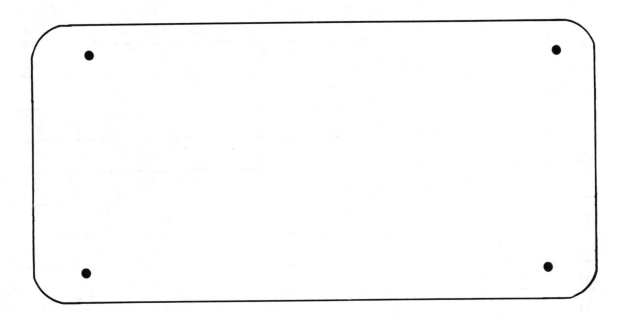

On a separate piece of paper, create a license plate that in some way describes you! For example, if your hobby is geology, your license plate might say ROCKY! If you enjoy making cakes, it might say BAKER. If bowling is your favorite sport you might want to use a bowling term. Remember to use no more that six numbers and/or letters!

41

A NEW NEIGHBOR

Pretend that a child from the state of _____
has moved to your neighborhood recently. What are the main
problems that he or she will have to face? What are the ways
in which you might help your new neighbor overcome the problems?
Write your ideas on the bottom of this page.

POSSIBLE PROBLEMS

1. _____

_____

2. _____

_____

3. _____

_____

4. _____

_____

5. _____

_____

HOW I CAN HELP

1. _____

_____

2. _____

_____

3. _____

_____

4. _____

_____

5. _____

_____

Educational Impressions, Inc.

CATEGORIES QUIZ

In fifteen minutes, try to fill in as many spaces as you can in the grid below. You may put more than one answer in each block. Try to think of unusual answers and you will score more points! Some examples are done for you.

	CITIES	GEOGRAPHICAL FEATURES	NATIONAL PARKS	FAMOUS PEOPLE
A				
M			MESA VERDE	
E				
R				REVERE
I				
C	CHICAGO			
A				

SCORE-1 point-common answer
2 points-unusual or only answer

NAME_____

Educational Impressions, Inc.

WHAT IF?

How might the history and development of our nation have been changed if certain important events had never occurred? Choose two of the following "What If" questions and provide your own thoughtful answers.

1. What if the United States had lost the Revolutionary War? How would our lives be different?

2. What if gold had not been discovered in California? How would the West have been settled?

3. What if Thomas Edison had never invented the light bulb? How would our lives be affected?

4. What if the Louisiana Territory had not been purchased? How might our history have been changed?

5. What if we did not have a Constitution to provide fair governing laws? How would our government function?

6. What if we had a king to rule our nation instead of an elected President?

Educational Impressions, Inc.

CHART YOUR ANSWERS!

Graphs and charts contain information that can be read quickly. One type of graph is called a <u>Pictograph</u>. In a pictograph, pictures are used in place of numbers. Look at the example below. It charts the grapefruit production of the U.S.A. Each grapefruit symbol represents 2,000,000 boxes of grapefruit. It is clear that Florida is the leading producer.

<u>GRAPEFRUIT</u>

Four Leading Grapefruit States

PICTOGRAPH

Another type of graph is called the <u>Bar Graph</u>. This type of graph can be used to show a great variety of facts. The example below shows the amount of oil production in the leading states. The numbers on the left indicate millions of barrels.

OIL PRODUCTION

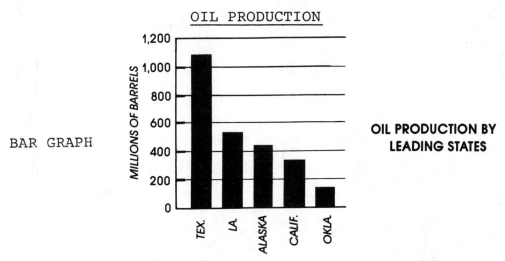

BAR GRAPH

Can you create your own graph to show information? Use facts from your research about your state or compare several states. Do your work on another paper.

DESIGN A STAMP

Stamps often provide us with a unique glimpse of our American heritage. On this page, you are asked to design a stamp that will reflect your state in some way. You may choose to honor an event, place or person of historical importance or to create a stamp that would portray a recent event or achievement in your state.

Educational Impressions, Inc.

Creative Thinking

MAKE A WORD PICTURE

     Artists can create beautiful pictures with paint and brush! Writers can create beautiful pictures with words! In this activity, you are asked to use your imagination and research information to create original word pictures of the state that you are studying.

Examples:

    1. White clapboard villages, nestled between high, tree-covered mountains and clear blue lakes

    2. Vast swampy grasslands and long sandy beaches with palm trees swaying in the sun.

What states do the above word pictures describe?

List six word pictures below. Create two for your own research state. Create four for other states of your choice.

WORD PICTURES   NAME OF STATE

1. _____

_____

2. _____

_____

3. _____

_____

4. _____

_____

5. _____

_____

6. _____

_____

Educational Impressions, Inc.

HIDDEN STATE AND CITY PUZZLE

Can you find the hidden states and cities in the sentences on this page? They are: Vermont, Maine, Idaho, Alaska, Colorado, Iowa, Oregon, Utah, Butte, Denver, Reno, Salem, Dover, and Dayton.

The first one is done for you. Be sure to underline your answers.

1. The rad<u>io wa</u>s turned off.
2. The main event was held in a stadium.
3. Do you always butter your bread?
4. It was a foregone conclusion that we would win the game.
5. The sale merchandise was purchased quickly.
6. Color adobe houses red.
7. There are no more pencils in the desk.
8. Put a horse in a stable.
9. Ron did a homework assignment incorrectly.
10. She cared for her garden very well.
11. Did Al ask a foolish question?
12. Today, Tony is celebrating his birthday.
13. Over months of time, the flowers grew.
14. The song was played over and over again.

Try to create your own hidden state or city sentences. Write them in the space below and exchange with a classmate to solve.

JOB SEARCH

Many occupations depend upon the geography, industry, climate, or natural resources of each state. For example, a ski instructor would likely find work in the states of Colorado or Vermont, while a grape grower would find fertile fields for his vineyards in sunny California. In ten minutes, see how many occupations you can list that match each special environment!

STATE	OCCUPATION

1.

2.

3.

4.

5.

6.

7.

8.

9.

10.

11.

12.

Educational Impressions, Inc.

Pennsylvania pleases people!

ALLITERATIONS ARE FUN!

An alliteration is created by using the same sound at the beginning of consecutive words such as:

INDIANA IS INVITING!

PENNSYLVANIA PLEASES PEOPLE!

Using state names, create your own alliteration sentences using three or more words in each.

1.

2.

3.

4.

5.

6.

7.

8.

9.

10.

11.

12.

Educational Impressions, Inc.

CREATE A TRAVEL POSTER!

Pretend that you work for a tour company. It is your job to design a travel poster that will attract tourists to the state of _____. Use your research information to help you plan your poster. You will want to include the outstanding attractions of the state. Arrange your poster creatively! Include the name of the state.

YOUR TRAVEL POSTER

MAKE A MENU!

Throughout our nation, people enjoy a variety of regional foods. For example, in Louisiana, you might try some delicious Creole cooking, and if you travel to Maine, you might indulge in a tasty lobster dinner! Many states give different names to the same foods. A submarine sandwich is also called a grinder (Vermont) or a hoagie (Eastern Pennsylvania). On this page, create a menu of some of the favorite regional foods in your research state. In some states, this may vary from city to city. After you have created your menu, share it with your classmates and compare the results.

MENU

FOR THE STATE OF _____

BREAKFAST FOODS

DINNER FOODS

LUNCH FOODS

SNACKS

DRINKS

CLASSIFY THE STATES!

How many ways can you group the states listed on this page? Consider the size, location, climate, geographical features, spelling, etc. There are many unusual possibilities. List your groupings on the bottom of the page, and give each group a title!

FLORIDA	TENNESSEE	HAWAII
DELAWARE	NEW JERSEY	ARIZONA
KENTUCKY	COLORADO	MONTANA
CALIFORNIA	SOUTH DAKOTA	GEORGIA
WYOMING	KANSAS	NEVADA
NEW YORK	OHIO	MICHIGAN
MAINE	RHODE ISLAND	ALASKA
TEXAS	IDAHO	VERMONT

EXAMPLE: <u>ALL HAVE TWO WORDS</u>

NEW JERSEY
SOUTH DAKOTA
RHODE ISLAND
NEW YORK

<u>YOUR GROUPS!</u>

CIRCLE YOUR MOST UNUSUAL GROUP IDEA!

53

Educational Impressions, Inc.

GUESS THE STATE

```
V  I  I  T  H
I  A  E  N  N
M  O  S  A  E
W  A  X  J  F
```

1. Cross out the letters of the state whose nickname is the Hawkeye State.
2. Cross out the first letter of the Green Mountain State.
3. Cross out the first and last letters of the 50th state.
4. Cross out all the letters of the biggest oil producing state.
5. Cross out the abbreviation of the Garden State.
6. Cross out the first letter of the state that has the Everglades Park in it.

What state is left?

Educational Impressions, Inc.

Section IV: States Fair

PRODUCT MAP DISPLAY

Look up the information on your state product map
from the Map Skills Section of the book. Collect as many of the
state's important products, raw materials, or pictures of them
as you can. Attach the products to the correct map location by
using colored string or ribbon and tape as shown below. Use this
display on your exhibit table.

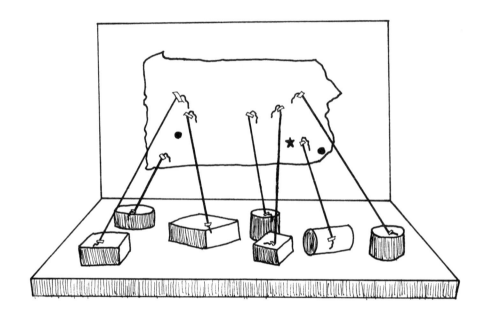

List the products that will appear on your table.

1.

2.

3.

4.

5.

6.

SHARE YOUR KNOWLEDGE

In preparation for the States Fair, you are responsible for making a handout that will show some of the information that you have obtained from your research. Look in the other sections of the book for ideas on products such as newsletters, fact sheets, puzzles, travel posters and product maps. Be creative and come up with an original idea! Duplicate your handout, and share it with others on the day of the States Fair! On this page, list some ideas that you might develop into informative handouts.

1.

2.

3.

4.

5.

6.

7.

8.

CIRCLE YOUR BEST IDEAS!

BE A SPEECH WRITER

A very important part of the States Fair will be the presentation of a short speech describing the highlights of your research state. You may choose to relate any facts that you think are important and that the visitors to the fair will find interesting. A sample speech might start . . .

"Hello! My research state is Alabama. Alabama is known as the "Heart of Dixie" state because of its location. It became our 22nd state in 1819. Alabama grows more cotton than any other crop."

Compose your speech on the bottom of this page. Refer to your research sheets for ideas and information. Besure to include at least six or more important facts in your speech.

_____

_____

_____

_____

_____

_____

_____

_____

_____

_____

_____

_____

_____

Educational Impressions, Inc.

MY STATE EXHIBIT PLANNING SHEET

BY_____

MY STATE IS_____

DATE OF EXHIBIT_____

TIME_____ PLACE_____

BELOW IS A LIST OF THINGS THAT I WILL NEED FOR MY DISPLAY:

_____   _____

_____   _____

_____   _____

_____   _____

_____   _____

_____   _____

BELOW IS A SKETCH OF THE WAY I WILL DISPLAY MY THINGS AT THE EXHIBIT

you
are
here

CREATE A PROJECT

You might want to include a creative project on your exhibit table. The project should reflect the results of your research in some way. Here is a list of project ideas.

CLAY MODEL	TRAVELOGUE	FILMSTRIP
CREATIVE GAME	MOBILE	POEM BOOKLET
COLLAGE	MAP	BOOK
CARTOON BOOK	FLIP BOOK	PHOTOGRAPH DISPLAY
BROCHURE	DEMONSTRATION	PROJECT CUBE
LEARNING CENTER	NEWSPAPER	ORIGINAL SONG
TAPE	RADIO SHOW	SLIDE SHOW
MURAL	MAGAZINE	COMMERCIAL
DICTIONARY	COMPUTER PRINT OUT	SILKSCREEN

On the botton of this page, list some of your project ideas. Describe the information that they might contain. Example:

PROJECT IDEA   TYPE OF INFORMATION

1. Creative Game-"Travel To   Geography and history
    Tennessee"   of Tennessee.

Educational Impressions, Inc.

RESEARCH CHART

On this page, you will find a research chart plan for your state information. Use this sample chart for your first draft. A larger copy of this can be placed on the front of your exhibit table with pictures highlighting various features of your study.

RESEARCH CHART FOR THE STATE OF:_____

Use your research section activity pages to discover as many important facts as you can about your state. You may add on extra lines for more topics.

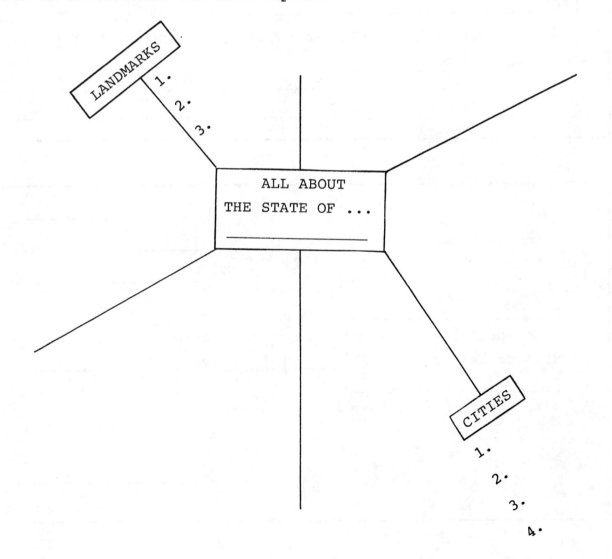

Educational Impressions, Inc.

INVITATIONS

You may select either of the two invitation forms below to invite visitors to your fair or you may write your own.

YOU ARE INVITED TO OUR STATES FAIR!

DATE:_____

TIME:_____

PLACE:_____

    WE HOPE THAT YOU WILL ENJOY IT AND BECOME MORE INFORMED ABOUT OUR NATION!

                LOVE,

             _____

             _____

             _____

             _____

Dear_____,

    We would like to invite you to come to our States Fair. It will be held on _____ at _____ in _____.

    We hope you will have a super time!

                Love,

             _____

THANK YOU NOTE

_____

_____

_____

DEAR_____,

    THANK YOU FOR ALL OF YOUR HELP AND COOPERATION IN
MAKING OUR STATES FAIR EXHIBIT A BIG SUCCESS! OUR CLASS
REALLY APPRECIATED YOUR EFFORTS. WE HOPE THAT YOU ENJOYED
VISITING OUR FAIR AND ADDED TO YOUR KNOWLEDGE OF OUR NATION.

                      LOVE,

                      _____

                      AND CLASS

(SIGN CLASS NAMES BELOW)

Educational Impressions, Inc.

Certificate

This is to certify that

_____

has done an outstanding job with

state exhibit

_____

all about the state of

_____

Date _____ Signed _____

SEAL

EVALUATION

The evaluation sheets on this page may be duplicated and distributed to visitors as they complete their tour of the States Fair.

OUR STATES FAIR

1. Did you enjoy our exhibits?_____

2. Name your favorite exhibit._____

3. Name one special thing that you learned from attending the fair. _____

4. Would you like to see another exhibit of this kind?_____

DATE_____NAME (OPTIONAL)_____

OUR STATES FAIR

1. Which state did you enjoy learning about the most?_____

2. What new fact did you learn about this state?_____
_____

3. Name some outstanding projects that you saw at the exhibit.
_____

4. What was your favorite handout at this exhibit?_____
_____

DATE_____NAME (OPTIONAL)_____

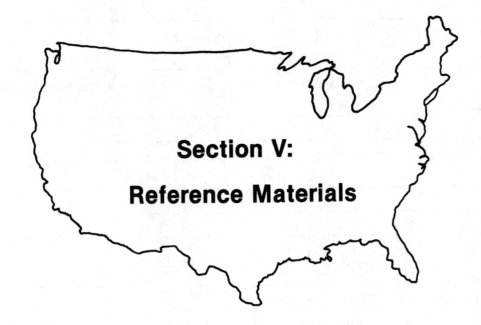

Section V:

Reference Materials

Educational Impressions, Inc.

JOURNEY AROUND THE NATION
PRE-TEST

1. In ten minutes, name as many states of the United States as you can!_____

    _____

    _____

    _____

2. Name at least five national landmarks. _____

    _____

3. Name at least six large rivers or lakes in the United States. _____

    _____

4. Match ten states with their capital cities! _____

    _____

    _____

    _____

5. Name five national parks. _____

    _____

6. Which was the first state? _____the last? _____
7. List five different types of maps. _____

    _____

    _____

8. Name the highest spot in the United States._____

    _____

9. Name the lowest spot in the United States. _____

    _____

10. Name three major industries of the Midwest. _____

    _____

11. Name the Time Zones of the United States. _____

    _____

    _____

68

JOURNEY AROUND THE NATION
SIMULATION GAME

1. A large United States map with mileage equivalent should be placed on a classroom bulletin board before beginning game.

2. Using SELECTION PAGE, each student chooses a "Home or Research State." If class is large, students may work in small groups.

3. Each student designs a marker that is symbolic of his state. (landmark, product etc.) This marker will be used to show each stop along the route. It can be pinned or taped to the map.

4. Students are required to complete activities from:
   SECTION I   - Maps
   SECTION II   - Research
   SECTION III - Creative Thinking
   As students complete activity pages, they receive points which convert into miles.

5. Scoring-Each completed activity page is equal to 5 points or 250 miles. However, the teacher may deduct points if the product is unsatisfactory or add points if the product is superior.

1 point=50 miles	6 points=300 miles
2 points=100 miles	7 points=350 miles
3 points=150 miles	8 points=400 miles
4 points=200 miles	9 points=450 miles
5 points=250 miles	10 points=500 miles

6. On the SCORING PAGE, the teacher may keep a record of each student's travel points. The sheet may be duplicated and placed on the bulletin board near the map.

7. Transportation-Each student is required to use at least 5 different types of transportation during his journey. He must keep a record of transportation used during his journey on the scoring sheet.

8. Detour Cards-After 1,000 miles of travel, each student selects a Detour Card. These cards may be duplicated and attached to heavy cardboard for classroom use. Students may create additional Detour Cards to be used in the game.

9. Bonus Points-Bonus points for extra credit projects may be awarded by the teacher. Examples:
   MODELS-5 points
   REPORTS-5 points
   CREATIVE POEMS AND STORIES-5 points

10. The first student to travel around the nation is the winner of the game. The teacher may require all students to accumulate a minimum amount of points before ending the game and proceeding on to the States Fair.

Educational Impressions, Inc.

1. EARTHQUAKE!!
   Many trees and wires are down. Do not move this turn. Conditions are dangerous.

2. FLOODED ROADS!!
   Roads are flooded in all directions! You must go back 100 miles!

3. TRAFFIC VIOLATION!!
   Your vehicle was going the wrong way on the highway. Local police have stopped you! Travel only 25 miles this turn.

4. VOLCANO DANGER!!
   A volcano is about to erupt! Go back 100 miles to be safe!

5. TYPHOON AHEAD!!
   Stay where you are for your own protection! Do not move this turn!

6. LOST LUGGAGE!!
   Luggage must be replaced at this stop! You must miss this turn!

7. SEVERE RAINSTORMS
   Many trees and wires are down. You are unable to travel at this time. Miss this turn!

8. AIRLINE STRIKE!!
   There are no flights out of this stop today! You may travel 100 miles by land.

9. SHIP REPAIRS NEEDED!!
   No water transportation! You may travel 100 miles by land today!

10. DENSE FOG!!
    All transportation is halted today due to the weather. Miss this turn.

11. TRAINS DERAILED TODAY!!
    NO travel by train is allowed today. You may use water transportation for 150 miles, if possible.

12. BUS TERMINAL CLOSED!!
    All bus transportation is halted for today. You may travel by air for 200 miles.

13. AVALANCHE!!
    All roads out are blocked! All airports are closed! You must miss this turn!

14. OUT OF GAS!!
    Your car ran out of gas on the highway. You will be delayed. Travel only 50 miles this turn!

70

15. ROAD REPAIRWORK
There are detours in all directions! Go back 50 miles!

16. SHIPWRECK!!
Your ship is caught in a storm!! Abandon ship and travel 50 miles north when you reach land!

17. BLIZZARD!!
Record breaking snowfall has brought all transportation to a halt! You may not travel this turn.

18. ICY ROADS!
Travel is very dangerous. You may only travel 50 miles this turn.

19. BRIDGE COLLAPSED!
You must go back 25 miles!

20. HAILSTORM!!
You must wait for the storm to pass. Only travel 25 miles this turn.

21. FENDER BENDER!
You have witnessed a minor accident. You lose a lot of travel time. Only proceed 10 miles this turn.

22. POLICE BARRACADE!
The police are questioning everyone who passes. You may travel only 50 miles this turn.

23. FLAT TIRE!
You must stop to fix your flat tire. Travel only 50 miles this turn.

24. PARADE!
A very long parade is blocking your passage. You must wait for it to pass. Travel only 100 miles this turn.

Educational Impressions, Inc.

SCORING SHEET

JOURNEY AROUND THE NATION

STUDENT NAME	HOME STATE	POINTS ACCUMULATED	MILES ACCUMULATED	TRANSPORTATION	LAST STOP

STATEHOOD INFORMATION

STATE	YEAR SETTELD	YEAR OF ADMISSION
ALABAMA	1702	1819
ALASKA	1784	1959
ARIZONA	1848	1912
ARKANSAS	1785	1836
CALIFORNIA	1769	1850
COLORADO	1858	1876
CONNECTICUT	1635	1788
DELAWARE	1638	1787
FLORIDA	1565	1845
GEORGIA	1733	1788
HAWAII		1959
IDAHO	1842	1890
ILLINOIS	1720	1818
INDIANA	1733	1816
IOWA	1788	1846
KANSAS	1727	1861
KENTUCKY	1774	1792
LOUISIANA	1699	1812
MAINE	1624	1820
MARYLAND	1834	1788
MASSACHUSETTS	1620	1788
MICHIGAN	1668	1837
MINNESOTA	1805	1858
MISSISSIPPI	1699	1817
MISSOURI	1735	1821
MONTANA	1809	1889
NEBRASKA	1847	1867
NEVADA	1850	1864
NEW HAMPSHIRE	1623	1788
NEW JERSEY	1664	1787
NEW MEXICO	1605	1912
NEW YORK	1614	1788
NORTH CAROLINA	1650	1789
NORTH DAKOTA	1766	1889
OHIO	1788	1803
OKLAHOMA	1889	1907
OREGON	1811	1859
PENNSYLVANIA	1682	1787
RHODE ISLAND	1636	1790
SOUTH CAROLINA	1670	1788
SOUTH DAKOTA	1856	1889
TENNESSEE	1757	1796
TEXAS	1691	1845
UTAH	1847	1896
VERMONT	1724	1791
VIRGINIA	1607	1788
WASHINGTON	1811	1889
WEST VIRGINIA	1727	1863
WISCONSIN	1766	1848
WYOMING	1834	1890

73

Educational Impressions, Inc.

STATE CAPITALS

STATE	CAPITAL CITY
ALABAMA	MONTGOMERY
ALASKA	JUNEAU
ARIZONA	PHOENIX
ARKANSAS	LITTLE ROCK
CALIFORNIA	SACRAMENTO
COLORADO	DENVER
CONNECTICUT	HARTFORD
DELAWARE	DOVER
FLORIDA	TALLAHASSEE
GEORGIA	ATLANTA
HAWAII	HONOLULU
IDAHO	BOISE
ILLINOIS	SPRINGFIELD
INDIANA	INDIANAPOLIS
IOWA	DES MOINES
KANSAS	TOPEKA
KENTUCKY	FRANKFORT
LOUISIANA	BATON ROUGE
MAINE	AUGUSTA
MARYLAND	ANNAPOLIS
MASSACHUSETTS	BOSTON
MICHIGAN	LANSING
MINNESOTA	ST. PAUL
MISSISSIPPI	JACKSON
MISSOURI	JEFFERSON CITY
MONTANA	HELENA
NEBRASKA	LINCOLN
NEVADA	CARSON CITY
NEW HAMPSHIRE	CONCORD
NEW JERSEY	TRENTON
NEW MEXICO	SANTE FE
NEW YORK	ALBANY
NORTH CAROLINA	RALEIGH
NORTH DAKOTA	BISMARCK
OHIO	COLUMBUS
OKLAHOMA	OKLAHOMA CITY
OREGON	SALEM
PENNSYLVANIA	HARRISBURG
RHODE ISLAND	PROVIDENCE
SOUTH CAROLINA	COLUMBIA
SOUTH DAKOTA	PIERRE
TENNESSEE	NASHVILLE
TEXAS	AUSTIN
UTAH	SALT LAKE CITY
VERMONT	MONTPELIER
VIRGINIA	RICHMOND
WASHINGTON	OLYMPIA
WEST VIRGINIA	CHARLESTON
WISCONSIN	MADISON
WYOMING	CHEYENNE

ORIGINAL THIRTEEN STATES

CONNECTICUT
DELAWARE
GEORGIA
MARYLAND
MASSACHUSETTS
NEW HAMPSHIRE
NEW JERSEY
NEW YORK
NORTH CAROLINA
PENNSYLVANIA
RHODE ISLAND
SOUTH CAROLINA
VIRGINIA

Educational Impressions, Inc.

STATE NICKNAMES

ALABAMA: THE HEART OF DIXIE
ALASKA: THE LAST FRONTIER
ARIZONA: THE GRAND CANYON STATE
ARKANSAS: THE LAND OF OPPORTUNITY
CALIFORNIA: THE GOLDEN STATE
COLORADO: THE CENTENNIAL STATE
CONNECTICUT: THE CONSTITUTION STATE
DELAWARE: THE DIAMOND STATE; THE FIRST STATE
FLORIDA: THE SUNSHINE STATE
GEORGIA: THE EMPIRE STATE OF THE SOUTH; THE PEACH STATE
HAWAII: THE ALOHA STATE
IDAHO: THE GEM STATE
ILLINOIS: THE LAND OF LINCOLN; THE PRAIRIE STATE
INDIANA: THE HOOSIER STATE
IOWA: THE HAWKEYE STATE
KANSAS: THE SUNFLOWER STATE
KENTUCKY: THE BLUEGRASS STATE
LOUISIANA: THE PELICAN STATE
MAINE: THE PINE TREE STATE
MARYLAND: THE OLD LINE STATE
MASSACHUSETTS: THE BAY STATE
MICHIGAN: THE WOLVERINE STATE
MINNESOTA: THE GOPHER STATE
MISSISSIPPI: THE MAGNOLIA STATE
MISSOURI: THE SHOW ME STATE
MONTANA: THE TREASURE STATE
NEBRASKA: THE CORN HUSKER STATE
NEVADA: THE SILVER STATE
NEW HAMPSHIRE: THE GRANITE STATE
NEW JERSEY: THE GARDEN STATE
NEW MEXICO: THE LAND OF ENCHANTMENT
NEW YORK: THE EMPIRE STATE
NORTH CAROLINA: THE TARHEEL STATE
NORTH DAKOTA: THE FLICKERTAIL STATE
OHIO: THE BUCKEYE STATE
OKLAHOMA: THE SOONER STATE
OREGON: THE BEAVER STATE
PENNSYLVANIA: THE KEYSTONE STATE
RHODE ISLAND: LITTLE RHODY
SOUTH CAROLINA: THE PALMETTO STATE
SOUTH DAKOTA: COYOTE STATE; SUNSHINE STATE
TENNESSEE: THE VOLUNTEER STATE
TEXAS: THE LONE STAR STATE
UTAH: THE BEEHIVE STATE
VERMONT: THE GREEN MOUNTAIN STATE
VIRGINIA: THE OLD DOMINION STATE
WASHINGTON: THE EVERGREEN STATE

WEST VIRGINIA: THE MOUNTAIN STATE
WISCONSIN: THE BADGER STATE
WYOMING: THE EQUALITY STATE

Handout Sample

PENNSYLVANIA

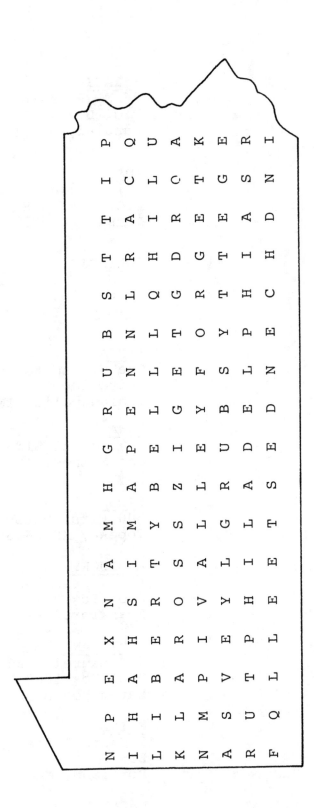

SEEK AND FIND

Amish	Gettysburg	Philadelphia	Ross
Erie	Liberty Bell	Pittsburg	Steel
Franklin	Penn	Quaker	Valley Forge

CHAMBER OF COMMERCE DIRECTORY

ALABAMA
468 S. Perry Street
P.O. Box 76
Montgomery, AL 36195

ALASKA
310 Second Street
Juneau, AK 99801

ARIZONA
3216 N. Third Street
Suite 103
Phoenix, AZ 85012

ARKANSAS
911 Wallace Street
Little Rock, AR 72201

CALIFORNIA
1027 Tenth Street
P.O. Box 1736
Sacramento, CA 95808

COLORADO
225 W. Colfax Avenue
Denver, CO 80202

CONNECTICUT
250 Constitution Plaza
Hartford, CT 06103

DELAWARE
One Commerce Center
Wilmington, DE 19801

DISTRICT OF COLUMBIA
1133 15th Street NW
Room 620
Washington, DC 20005

FLORIDA
136 Bronough Street
P.O. Box 11309
Tallahassee, FL 32302

GEORGIA
575 N. Omni International
Atlanta, GA 30335

HAWAII
26 N. Puunene Avenue
P.O. Box 1677
Kahului, HI 96732

IDAHO
711 W. Bannock Street
P.O. Box 2368
Boise, ID 83701

ILLINOIS
20 No. Walker Drive
Suite 1960
Chicago, IL 60606

INDIANA
One N. Capitol Street
Suite 200
Indianapolis, IN 46204

IOWA
250 Jewett Bldg.
Des Moines, IO 50309

KANSAS
500 First National Bank
Topeka, KS 66603

KENTUCKY
452 Versailles Road
P.O. Box 817
Frankfort, KY 40601

LOUISIANA
564 Laurel Road
P.O. Box 1868
Baton Rouge, LA 70821

MAINE
1 Canal Plaza
Box 65
Portland, ME 04112

MARYLAND
60 West Street
Suite 405
Annapolis, MD 21401

CHAMBER OF COMMERCE DIRECTORY

MASSACHUSETTS
100 Cambridge Street
Boston, MA 02202

MICHIGAN
200 N. Washington Square
Suite 400
Lansing, MI 48933

MINNESOTA
419 N. Robert Street
240 Bremer Bldg.
St. Paul, MN 55101

MISSISSIPPI
P.O. Box 1849
Jackson, MS 39205

MISSOURI
428 E. Capitol Street
P.O. Box 149
Jefferson City, MO 65102

MONTANA
110 Neill Avenue
P.O. Box 1730
Helena, MT 59024

NEBRASKA
P.O. Box 81556
Lincoln, NE 68501

NEVADA
P.O. Box 2806
Reno, NV 89505

NEW HAMPSHIRE
State House Annex
P.O. Box 856
Concord, NH 03301

NEW JERSEY
State House Annex
P.O. Box 856
Newark, NJ 07102

NEW MEXICO
P.O. Box 25100
Albuquerque, NM 87125

NEW YORK
152 Washington Avenue
Albany, NY 12210

NORTH CAROLINA
201 N. Roxboro Street
Durham, NC 27701

NORTH DAKOTA
808 Third Street
P.O. Box 2467
Fargo, ND 58108

OHIO
17 S. High Street
8th Floor
Columbus, OH 43215

OKLAHOMA
4020 N. Lincoln Blvd.
Oklahoma City, OK 73105

OREGON
P.O. Box 696
Gresham, OR 97030

PENNSYLVANIA
222 N. Third Street
Harrisburg, PA 17101

RHODE ISLAND
91 Park Street
Providence, RI 02908

SOUTH CAROLINA
Bankers Trust Tower
Suite 520
1301 Gervais Street
P.O. Box 11278
Columbia, SC 29211

SOUTH DAKOTA
300 S. Highland Street
P.O. Box 548
Pierre, SD 57501

TENNESSEE
161 Fourth Avenue
Nashville, TN 37219

TEXAS
1012 Perry Brooks Blvd.
Austin, TX 78701

UTAH
19 E. Second Street
Salt Lake City, UT 84111

VERMONT
Granger Road
P.O. Box 37
Montpelier, VT 05602

VIRGINIA
611 E. Franklin Street
Richmond, VA 23219

WASHINGTON
1200 One Union Square
Seattle, WA 98101

WEST VIRGINIA
1101 Kanawha Valley Bldg.
P.O. Box 2789
Charleston, WV 25330

WISCONSIN
111 E. Wisconsin Drive
Milwaukee, WI 53202

WYOMING
301 W. 16th Street
P.O. Box 1147
Cheyenne, WY 82003